Pocket

Bach Flowers

Susan Holden

Astrolog Publishing House

Pocket Healing Books

Holistic Healing
Dr. Ilona Melman

Aromatherapy
Kevin Hudson

Reiki
Chantal Dupont

Vitamins
Jon Tillman

Bach Flowers
Susan Holden

Herbal Remedies
Dan Wolf

Minerals
Jon Tillman

Color Healing
Barbara White

This publication contains the opinions and ideas of its author. It is intended to provide helpful and informative material on the subject matter covered. It is sold with the understanding that the authors and publisher are not engaged in rendering professional services in the book. If the reader requires personal assistance or advice, a competent professional should be consulted.

The author, book producer, and publisher specifically disclaim any responsibility for any liability, loss or risk, personal or otherwise, which is incurred as a consequence, directly or indirectly, of the use and application of any of the contents of this book.

Introduction

Bach Flower Remedies were devised by a British general practitioner in the first third of the 20th century. Dr. Edward Bach, who was born in 1886, had a large general medical practice. Over the years, he discerned a certain trend among his patients: When they were in some kind of stressful or anxiety-provoking situation, they suffered from a wide range of symptoms. As a responsible and cautious GP, Dr. Bach would carefully treat these symptoms. However, he began to realize that although the patients were gaining a certain amount of symptomatic relief, he was not actually getting to the very root of their problems, which, in general, lay in the psychological realm.

Dr. Bach reached the conclusion that body and mind were an interreacting entity, and that the patient's psychological condition exerted a substantial influence on his physical state: in other words, one aspect could not be treated without relating to the other. If the root of the problem is treated, the ailment will be cured far more effectively than if just the symptoms are treated. Dr. Bach maintained that if symptomatic treatment alone was administered, the basic problem would remain, and the disease would never really be eradicated. He decided that the solution to this "body-mind" treatment problem lay in plants. He began to study homeopathy and pharmacology, specializing in flowers, and classifying them according to their effect on the psychological conditions that lay at the root of many illnesses. His first set of extracts was called "The Twelve Healers."

In the 1930s, Dr. Bach devised a set of 38 flower extracts, or remedies divided into seven categories according to the particular emotional disorder for which each one was suitable. He laid down precise ground rules for diagnosing the illnesses, and provided instructions for the production and dosage of the remedies.

Dr. Bach's "rescue package" consisted of five extracts, to be used in emergencies.

Bach Flower Remedies have no negative effects, and can be combined safely. The average dose is 2-4 drops diluted in water, three times a day, or applied directly to the skin.

The extracts are numbered according to the alphabetical order of the names of the flowers.

Name of Patient

1. Agrimony
2. Aspen
3. Beech
4. Centaury
5. Cerato
6. Cherry Plum
7. Chestnut Bud
8. Chicory
9. Clematis
10. Crab Apple
11. Elm
12. Gentian
13. Gorse
14. Heather
15. Holly
16. Honeysuckle
17. Hornbeam
18. Impatiens
19. Larch
20. Mimulus
21. Mustard

22. Oak
23. Olive
24. Pine
25. Red Chestnut
26. Rock Rose
27. Rock Water
28. Seleranthus
29. Star of Bethlehem
30. Sweet Chestnut
31. Vervain
32. Vine
33. Walnut
34. Water Violet
35. White Chestnut
36. Wild Oat
37. Wild Rose
38. Willow
39. Rescue Remedy

1. Agrimony

Agrimony is appropriate for people who are prone to deep suffering and severe mental agony, but outwardly continue to smile and conceal their true state. These types can be the very people to whom everyone turns with their troubles, since they always provide a shoulder to cry on. While they are the life and soul of the party, and make everyone laugh, they are in fact in a poor mental or physical condition and need a shoulder or a helping hand. However, they will never reveal this fact to anyone.

This essence is also effective in situations of grief and loss, when the person has not managed to give vent to his pain and let it out, but continues to keep it pent up inside. These people sometimes tend to be afraid of being left alone or of having nothing to do, because they are unable to confront their emotions. They are also often afraid of vocal confrontations and arguments.

Agrimony can cause the person to feel like he's "taking off a mask," by evoking emotions and sometimes torrents of tears. This is a positive reaction, because these emotions needed to be released.

Physical symptoms: Ear and throat infections, sinus problems, chronic hoarseness, thyroid disorders, high blood pressure, and heart problems.

Characteristic sentences: "Everything's fine, wonderful." "Don't worry, I always get by."

2. Aspen

Aspen is used for treating fear or anxiety whose source is unknown. The physiological response to anxiety may be accelerated heartbeat, weakness, spasms, or tremor in the muscles, insomnia, cold sweat, and so forth.

There is probably a reason for the anxiety, but it is not conscious, and the patient is unable to define it. The sensation of fear is liable to appear in the company of other people, without rhyme or reason. When the anxiety is reduced, the patient is able to view his life more clearly, and to understand what is happening to him.

Possible physical symptoms: Cold sweat, weakness in the knees, accelerated heartbeat, rapid breathing, confused thought processes, vertigo, faintness, bladder infections, urinary incontinence, and impotence.

Aspen is a characteristic remedy for difficult periods in life and for periods in which the nervous system is upset or exhausted. It is also used in situations of weakness and muscular tremors resulting from excessive caffeine or (symptomatic) anorexia.

The essence soothes the patient, and when

his level of anxiety is reduced, he can look at his life clearly and understand what is happening to him.

3. Beech

Beech is appropriate for types who are critical and intolerant, and who cannot understand that everyone is born with different talents and chooses a different way of life. They are constantly criticizing people, seeing every flaw and everything that needs correcting (in their opinion), and they don't mince words about it. Nothing is ever "perfect" in their eyes. These types not only repress their emotions, but they are unaware of them; they are therefore incapable of understanding the emotions of others. They can be cynical and harsh to the point of negating the person opposite them. They are inclined to demand more of others than of themselves, and they seem to ignore their own faults. Sometimes they use humor to camouflage their criticism of strangers, but within the family circle, they can be lethal.

Often the source of this imbalance stems from having grown up under a microscope and being constantly criticized as children.

Physical symptoms: Various digestive problems, inflexibility in the skeletal system and the neck, joint problems, back problems, chronic constipation, and a general lack of flow in the body (because of their rigidity of thoughts and emotions, as well as their failure to go with the flow).

Characteristic sentences: "Why can't you be like the neighbors' son?" "How can you be so messy?"

The action of beech causes them to see themselves as they really are, creating a situation of introspection that can sometimes be rather shocking, but very positive.

4. Centaury

Centaury is for people who are extremely shy, and who go through life in the shadow of stronger and more dominant people without devoting energy to their own development. These people do not know how to say "no" and set limits. They tend to subjugate themselves voluntarily to people who are more forceful than they, and are consequently sometimes taken advantage of. They are inclined to place themselves last in the order of priorities, and allow other people to exploit them.

Centaury is also good for children who are weak and bashful, for premature babies, for states of recuperation after a long illness, when the person feels that he is incapable of making an effort , and for the recovery of the body after strict dieting. The essence can be fortifying for weak muscles or general weakness.

Characteristic sentences: "Don't pay any attention to me," "You don't have to worry about me."

Physical symptoms: Problems with the kidneys because of guilt feelings and fear, impotence, extreme fatigue, respiratory problems, pallor, dark rings under the eyes, stooped posture and a lack of energy, small weak babies, and premature infants.

The essence is known for "breaking bonds," and a person who has been like a browbeaten slave to others all his life can suddenly stand proudly erect.

5. Cerato

People of this type are drastically lacking in confidence in their knowledge and their decisions. They have a hard time making independent decisions, and tend to accept other people's opinions easily. They are extremely compulsive advice-seekers, hoard information obsessively, and are incapable of deciding what is correct. In spite of their extensive bank of information, they have difficulty applying it because of their lack of confidence in their internal knowledge and their failure to heed their inner voice. They are liable to change their mind time and time again, under the influence of other people's opinions. They can be very dependent, and admire people who take a stand, because of their lack of confidence in their own judgement. They find it difficult to concentrate on their studies because of their lack of confidence in their own knowledge. The result is an inability to decide based on a lack of confidence.

Cerato is also appropriate for any situation in which the person is unable to decide between various things, when he experiences temporary confusion, the feeling of standing at a crossroads without knowing which way to turn, a loss of inner identity, and a lack of confidence in personal knowledge.

Characteristic sentences: "I'm not sure, I don't understand." "I don't know and therefore I am incapable of deciding, or carrying out the task." "What do you think I should do?"

Physical symptoms: Tension headaches, lack of concentration, constant stress.

Cerato helps the person focus, and facilitates decision-making. It helps him know what he really wants.

6. Cherry Plum

Cherry plum is involved with the wholeness of the soul, with sanity, and with the fear of losing control. It is suitable for treating nervous breakdowns, an extreme lack of concentration, the fear of losing control, and the fear of going insane. Often, a Cherry Plum situation is characteristic of hormonal changes. Extreme cases include people who did in fact lose control and were hospitalized in psychiatric wards, and people who had a nervous breakdown because they gave up and could no longer cope with things.

Physical symptoms: All the phenomena of loss of control, such as loss of sphincter or bladder control, severe confusion, and anxieties.

Characteristic sentences: "If you don't restrain me, I'll kill him," "If I don't change jobs, I'm going to commit suicide." "I don't have the strength to keep on suffering." "I'm afraid I'll kill myself some day." "I feel like I'm going crazy." "I say and do things, but it isn't really me."

For all those who have lost control, cherry

plum pulls them together and centers them. At first, they are liable to lose control even more, in every way possible - more urination, more bowel movements, more crying, losing all sorts of things, not getting up on time in the mornings, and so on. Sometimes this lack of control frightens them enormously because of unanticipated things that occur, for example, unexpected guests suddenly show up - something that has never happened to them. Suddenly they become spontaneous and do things without planning them beforehand. The essence gradually centers them and induces a feeling of spiritual peace, while reducing their fear of losing their sanity. It gets them to see things in the proper perspective.

7. Chestnut Bud

Chestnut bud is a metamorphic essence that causes a return to the past and a move into the future, removing the hurdles so that the person can progress. This essence is characteristic of the type of people for whom the past has no meaning. They experience a lack of progress because they do not learn from the mistakes of the past, and tend to repeat them over and over again. For them, the experiences of the past are erased; each experience is isolated and is not connected to things that have happened before.

This essence constitutes learning - it teaches the person to bridge between the internal state, that is to say, the internal feeling, and the real conditions that prevail in his surroundings. Chestnut bud is also appropriate for people with learning disabilities and with emotional problems created while studying, and helps with memory problems as well.

Characteristic sentences are: "Every boss walks all over me." "Every man hits me." "In every job I get low wages."

Taking the essence is likely to make the person experience things he had long since forgotten - encounters with people from the past, and so on. The moment the experience reemerges, the person is granted an additional opportunity to examine it and learn from it.

8. Chicory

Chicory helps people who are overly focused on themselves, in addition to being materialistic and full of self-pity. Moreover, they don't know how to give unconditional love. These types are liable to subject others to emotional blackmail, "forcing" people to give them love, and expecting something back in return for everything they give. They can be manipulative, and arouse perpetual guilt feelings in those close to them. For example, they can be overprotective parents in the extreme, smothering their children with love and interfering in their lives incessantly. This situation frequently stems from a loveless childhood that has left the person with an inner vacuum that he is trying to fill by seeking recognition and affection from other people; he has a desperate fear of being abandoned. These types need constant attention, tend to be easily hurt or insulted, and demand respect. They see the world only in relation to themselves: "Whoever treats me nicely is 'good' and whoever does not is 'bad.'" Sometimes they are even capable of creating provocations and behaving in a negative manner, just to attract attention.

Physical symptoms: Stomach problems, problems with the liver and gall bladder, skin ailments, psoriasis, respiratory problems, asthma, bulimia.

Characteristic sentences: "I give you everything and you don't care about me." "Look what I've done for you." "Don't ask me why I'm hurt - you know why!"

Chicory gives a feeling of calmness, quiet, and space. Suddenly the person is able to make the connection between deeds and emotions, and sometimes the need to be alone arises, while the need for constant attention from those around him diminishes. The person feels more loved, and no longer searches for so much love from other people.

9. Clematis

Clematis is the essence for people who are "spaced out," whose head is in the clouds. Instead of dealing with life, they are immersed in daydreams, living in a fantasy future, and failing to deal with day-to-day life. They may be characterized by apathy, inertia, confusion, and forgetfulness due to lack of attention and fatigue resulting from boredom. There is always someone else who will assume the responsibility, since they cannot be relied on. They usually stick to someone who will do the job for them.

A Clematis type can fall asleep anywhere; adults escape into television and movies, women and girls vicariously live the lives of soap-opera heroes, around whom their entire existence revolves.

Clematis is also appropriate for the following situations: fainting and loss of consciousness; people described as "vegetable" can be treated with it, though it is rubbed on the forehead and temples rather than taken orally; people who engage in meditation and find it difficult to get back to earth; and all situations in which a person feels that he is not being practical. The most extreme case of the essence can be found in autism and in hyperactive children who are unable to concentrate.

The Clematis essence is also good for lack of concentration and attention deficit, and promotes concentration.

Physical symptoms: Slow and unfocused speech, staring eyes, weakness, faintness, a feeling of floating, a lack of stability in the feet, and any situation of being "uprooted" from the ground and reality in an exaggerated way.

This essence grounds a person and helps him become more practical and active in everyday life.

10. Crab Apple

Crab apple is an essence for physical and mental cleansing. It is appropriate for people who feel that they are "dirty" or "impure." In extreme instances, the imbalance can reach the point of compulsive cleanliness ("cleanliness freaks").

This essence is suitable for people who are revolted by bodily secretions and by sexual relations, who are ashamed of their bodies and attribute the negative properties of a lack of cleanness to them, and who consider themselves and their emotions to be ugly and unclean.

The essence can be used after situations that cause a person to feel sensations of disgust, such as opening a blocked sewer, visiting a hospital or any other place that leaves an unpleasant sensation (as though they have been contaminated by non-positive energies), and for purposes of cleansing the body in a state of fast and internal cleansing procedures, after prolonged use of medications, for external skin problems, for states of nasal congestion, mucus, blocked sinuses, for problems of revulsion at having sexual relations, and for cleansing and purifying physical wounds and cuts (both orally and externally - but not as a substitute for antiseptic substances). It is used for all infections of the blood, urine, throat, gums, and ears, as well as for bad breath. It is also used in mixtures for women who have suffered rape and feel polluted.

Physical symptoms: Compulsive hand-washing, revulsion for sheets, bedlinen, and any sort of secretion (blrth, menstruation, feces and urine, nursing). Among children, disgust for food and sheets is prominent.

Crab apple can also be applied externally: it is good for burns, eczema, fungal infections, psoriasis, and acne. The essence is also effective as a compress for the skin, and a few drops can also be placed in the bath. Used both externally and internally, it is very good for the treatment of bronchitis, throat infections, asthma, and all infections.

The essence is extremely effective as an aid in kicking habits such as overeating, smoking, alcohol, and so on).

11. Elm

This is a situational essence, appropriate for strong people who suddenly succumb to exhaustion, depression, and a lack of belief in themselves and in their ability to achieve their goals, people who assume a great deal of responsibility and suddenly become uncertain as to whether they are making the right decisions. The people who live with this type are astounded, as they are used to seeing him functioning at full steam, and making decisions with no hesitation. The person himself will say, out of sheer exhaustion, "I can't think straight," and the decision he makes is liable to be incorrect. This situation is also true of the mother who was always strong and functioned well and has suddenly stopped doing so, strong friends who suddenly break down, and a manager who is facing an important decision and suddenly becomes unsure of his judgement. Fortunately, this is a brief and temporary situation - these people recover quickly and return to their normal behavior.

Elm is also appropriate for moments of crisis in which we feel that we can't meet other people's expectations, and they will be hurt as a result.

Bach said: "Take care of yourself - take a break occasionally and go away on holiday."

Physical symptoms: Severe exhaustion, fatigue, sudden and uncharacteristic dependency.

12. Gentian

This essence is for people who are pessimistic and depressive, and see only the gloomy side of life. The Gentian type's depression and despair always stem from a known cause. This essence belongs to the pessimistic type of person; it is one of the most negative and energetic masses possible.

His mottoes are: "There is no good without bad." "No pain, no gain." "Life is grim suffering." People of this type live the self-fulfilling prophecy; they beckon the negative energies with statements such as "It's not working," "It's not succeeding," and wherever they are, this is what happens.

Gentian helps this type during the treatment of illness as well by encouraging recovery.

Physical symptoms: The most common one is constipation. Gentian can be taken to alleviate it.

This essence helps people to see the "half-full glass," and to form a more optimistic view of the world.

13. Gorse

Bach described the appearance of Gorse type people thus: "With a pale yellowish cast and black lines under their eyes, they look like people who need some sun in their lives in order to shift the clouds above their heads."

Gorse is a caressing essence in the sense of cleansing the initial troubled atmosphere; it is an essence for people who are pessimistic by nature, people in despair, people who do not believe in others or in their ability to help them. They relate very suspiciously to anyone who tries to help them. They are in a state of deep, silent, internal despair; they do not speak out and express the feeling of "Enough! I can't take anymore." They are not suicidal, but they don't lift a finger to improve their situation. This is because the way they see it, there is nothing more to be done. These types conceal their feelings: "There's no point in talking about how I feel, because it won't help." They continue functioning under their burden of despair, saying to themselves: "I've already given up." Deep sadness can be perceived in them.

Gorse is a wonderful essence for people with

terminal diseases who are in despair, and for people who have experienced failure with another essence. It also helps people pull themselves out of despair, both giving them strength and ability, and helping them to learn the lesson that the difficult situation is meant to teach.

Among children, situations such as these are liable to occur - for example, when teachers or parents are on their backs, and they feel that their world has collapsed. "There's nothing that can be done about it. That's what life's all about."

Physical symptoms: All the phenomena that occur in states of depression.

Gorse brings light and hope, and the situation becomes more optimistic. While the problem has not changed, the essence affords the possibility of change.

14. Heather

Heather is an essence for treating people or conditions that have an enormous need of attention that is expressed in a very blatant manner - so much so that it feels as if people of this type are sucking the energy out of those around them. These types tell their acquaintances their entire life stories, not giving anyone else a chance to get a word in edgewise. They are incapable of understanding that enough is enough. In contrast to the Chicory type, who will be insulted, this type is never hurt, and continues to seek attention even after being rejected. This situation stems from the feeling of being unloved.

Physical symptoms: Obesity, a craving for sweet things, hypochondria, and many ailments that occur in order to attract attention.

15. Holly

Holly is used for treating people who suffer from negative feelings of hatred, anger, jealousy, rage, and loathing. People of this type do not believe that they are capable of being loved, so they project their negative emotions onto those around them. It is worth taking Holly in any situation in which one becomes extremely irritated. The Holly type is the embodiment of an emotional storm. It is most definitely an essence of love. These people are liable to embarrass people in public and even enjoy doing so, because of their own bitterness. The lack of balance can also be turned inward rather than outward, and then these people eat themselves up, since many situations and people cause them to experience negative feelings. They waste a lot of energy on anger and hatred.

Holly is also helpful in situations of divorce, in break-ups with a boy/girlfriend involving keen jealousy, or after an argument with someone, when that person's anger is not fading.

Physical symptoms: Children with problems

grinds to a halt. The essence helps the person cut loose from the past and get him to appreciate and enjoy the present.

16. Honeysuckle

Honeysuckle is appropriate for a situation or a type of person that is stuck in the past. Sometimes the person is not even aware of this fact. His key phrase is "When I was..." This situation sometimes occurs after a severe trauma, separation, or loss of someone close, when people return from abroad but are still there in spirit, and when people cannot stop thinking or talking about the things they could have done and the opportunities they have missed. Sometimes they live in the past and the future simultaneously, and pay no attention to the present.

Physical symptoms: Confusion, drowsiness, daydreaming.

Bach said of them: "All we have to do is to maintain our personality, live our lives, be the captains of our own ships, and everything will be fine."

Honeysuckle is also very good for people with Alzheimer's disease, as it improves their memory.

The essence is also good for any situation of stagnation and when the patient's progress of bedwetting and stuttering; gall bladder and liver problems; compulsive eating; constipation; blockages in the female sexual organs; clenching one's fists; grinding one's teeth.

17. Hornbeam

Hornbeam is an essence for a lack of motivation and the resulting mental and physical fatigue, for a lack of energy and *joie de vivre*. This essence is meant for people who find it hard to take the first step; they have a hard time in the mornings, or starting the week; it's hard for them to approach the boss and ask for a raise; they find it difficult to ask a girl out on a first date, and so on. For these people, the phrase "have to do" plunges them into despair and immobilizes them. The problem lies in taking the first step, and in their doubt in their ability to do so. After the first step, things work out by themselves.

Characteristic sentences: "I have to hand in a term paper, and just the thought of it is making me sick." "If I had a bit more strength in my legs, I would succeed." "I just can't get up in the morning and look at that paperwork on my desk." "I don't believe I'll be able to do that."

Physical symptoms: Headaches, backaches, pressure in the eyes, earaches, extreme fatigue, all the illnesses that result from the collapse of the immune system, or from ailments that prevent the person from beginning the task. The fatigue dissipates when the person takes an interest in what he is doing.

The essence fortifies the person and enables him to pick himself up and take the necessary step.

18. Impatiens

Impatiens is an essence for all situations that can be seen as situations of stress. The person lacks patience and tolerance; he feels that things are not moving at his rate; his thought processes work overtime - his head is constantly generating thoughts.

This essence is excellent for hyperactivity. Even when the person is physically calm, his thoughts race, and when he's physically hyperactive, he's calm in his thoughts. The energy surrounding him becomes nervous, and he feels that people around him are not acting or thinking quickly enough. His threshold of stimulation is very low, and he's very liable to have an outburst; his sympathetic system may be working all the time and therefore his stress mechanism is constantly functioning.

These people are sympathetic types (because the primary system at work is the sympathetic system. There may be a problem with acidity in the digestive system because the sympathetic system is working more). This type also needs to be learn to eat properly because his digestive system is also liable to cause overactivity of the sympathetic system.

They will probably suffer from an impaired digestive system. Because the energy is being channeled into stress, they do not breathe properly; their breathing is rapid, and their heart may not withstand the burden, leading to heart attacks. They are liable to suffer from high blood pressure, too.

They have a hard time lying in bed and resting; they burn up energy rapidly, and ultimately they experience extreme fatigue and a sudden drop in energy.

Physical symptoms: Nervous movements, problems with the digestive system, spasmodic pains, headaches, dermatological phenomena related to situations of stress, problems with the thyroid gland and with metabolism (the thyroid gland is associated with stress; a problem with the thyroid gland is only a symptom - generally speaking, the root of the problem resides in stress). Children can be very demanding, and want instant gratification. Women may experience a hormonal imbalance.

Impatiens is good for releasing knotted muscles - four drops an hour apart rubbed into the painful spot.

19. Larch

Larch is an essence for the most basic lack of confidence. The type is characterized by not doing things so as not to fail. He perceives failure as being the most frightening thing that can happen. When he has no choice, he is liable to do things in a way that will enable him to say later: "I told you not to do it like that." It is very typical of children who fail in school and then say, "I didn't study; if I'd studied, I would have passed." They have potential, but they don't see it. Their lack of confidence paralyzes them; they huddle in a corner and think that their opinion doesn't count, and that they don't have anything to say.

Characteristic sentences: "I can't." "I'm incapable." "I won't succeed." "I can't handle this." "I'm afraid of being in front of an audience." "I'm afraid of the boss."

Larch can also help with situations of stage fright and fear of heights (which can be an expression of the fear of failure). The person may feel inferior to others, and this gets him down.

The essence is also helpful in certain

situations, such as before an exam, appearing in front of an audience, or any other situation that can be perceived as a lack of confidence.

Physical symptoms: Weakness (body, muscles, skeleton, knees), voice loss, impotence, impaired virility.

20. Mimulus

Mimulus is an essence for the treatment of phobias and defined fears: elevators, the dark, dogs, closed places, bacteria, flying, old age, death, giving birth, pressure in day-to-day functioning, and so on.

As a type, these people are characterized as cowards: the fearful child, the cowardly adult, those who find it difficult to cope and are afraid of everything, children who cling to their parents' legs when a dog approaches (not out of hysteria), people who huddle fearfully together in an elevator. They may conceal their fear out of embarrassment.

Mimulus reduces the fear. It is a therapeutic essence and not an immediate one; the treatment works over time. Sometimes, after the fear has disappeared, the real reason for the fear emerges.

Physical symptoms: Similar to those of Aspen, but slightly weaker.

It can be given to babies who are easily startled, to people who experience pressure in the chest as a result of fear, and to people who suffer from impotence stemming from performance anxiety.

Mimulus helps to reduce the fear, and over time completely alleviates it. Along with losing the fear, the person may well understand the root of his fears.

21. Mustard

Mustard is used for treating severe depression that envelops the person like a black cloud. The person is liable to lose contact with reality and to remain in a state of deep sadness and inability to function. Symptoms such as severe depression, the need to sleep and escape, overeating, closing oneself off, irritability, a tendency to cry, a lack of will to cope, and a feeling of "I'm fed up with it" are liable to occur. The person plunges into depression for no apparent reason, and may well suffer from general gloominess and anxiety attacks.

Mustard should help depressions resulting from a hormonal imbalance (including depression during menstruation or ovulation) and problems with the thyroid gland.

Physical symptoms: Fatigue, exhaustion, heaviness.

This essence works quickly and effectively and helps the person get out of his depression, sometimes in an apparently extreme manner.

22. Oak

Oak is an essence for people who assume a great deal of responsibility, to the point of a physical and mental breakdown. This essence is appropriate for workaholics - people who go to work even when they're ill, convinced that nobody can manage without them. They take upon themselves tasks that others refuse to do. They see other people as being their responsibility as well. Their credo is that life is responsibility, a quest, an obligation, and theirs is the only way except to do things. They don't complain, because they feel that there isn't anyone else to take the responsibility - so they take it.

Oak people are very responsible - a great rock that can always be leaned on. With them, things are always well organized, and they do not leave work for others. They wear themselves out to the point of complete exhaustion.

People of this type do not usually complain, and will not say that they are unhappy, but they don't hide their troubles, either. They don't know how to rest and take a vacation. These are always the last things on their list of priorities.

Because they do not share responsibility with others, they are likely to reach breaking point - possibly a nervous breakdown.

Physical symptoms: Problems with the shoulders, neck, skeleton, slipped disc, and knees; ulcers and heart attacks. The greater their fatigue, the less their immune system functions, and then they pick up every disease that is going around. It is very common to find that they suffer from allergies.

Their body, which is already incapable of carrying the load, is liable to manifest the above symptoms in order to make them rest a bit. When Oak is experiencing a physical or emotional crash, it is good to administer Elm, since the essence is likely to "knock" the person into exhaustion that will force him to rest for a while. This reaction is a positive one because if the person does not rest, he can expect physical or mental collapse at a certain point.

23. Olive

Olive is an essence that helps the person cope with severe fatigue, total exhaustion, caused by the body's and mind's "decision" that there is an urgent need for rest. This situation is likely to arise from a long period of coping with mental or physical suffering, from severe sleep deprivation, and so on. The essence also helps in cases in which the person is recovering from a serious illness and is "addicted" to the feeling of exhaustion. The essence is also helpful for drops in energy level during the day. When one has to carry on functioning - for instance, after the after the midday break when someone tends to fall asleep as a result of physical exhaustion and tiredness, but he has an important meeting - taking three drops of Olive before the meeting will help him cope with the problem.

Olive is good for all cases in which the person wishes to increase his body's vitality, such as during exams, moving house, and so on.

Physical symptoms: A decrease in the functioning of the immune system as a result of fatigue - leading to flu, infections, and so on; also, any other symptom that indicates tiredness and exhaustion.

Olive can be administered in any situation requiring immediate energy; however, because the essence balances the body, if the person is in dire need of rest from a physical or mental point of view, the essence will "knock him out" so that he rests and enables his systems to recover.

24. Pine

Pine is an essence for guilt. As a type, this is a person who bears a perpetual feeling of guilt, taking the responsibility and blaming himself even for things that have nothing to do with him, to an extreme degree - the type of person who begs forgiveness for every little thing. This condition sometimes appears in children, because they tend to form guilt feelings about all sorts of things that they understand in an unrealistic manner (for instance, if their parents quarrel, they're convinced that it is because of them).

There are parents who manipulate their children by means of guilt ("You're ruining my health"), and severe guilt feelings are formed within the children - these are likely to continue into adulthood. The nature of a guilt feeling is that it requires punishment. If this does not come from without, people may punish themselves, and invite the punishment actively. For instance, "I will eat and stuff myself, and my punishment will be to become fat, disgusting, repulsive, and unpopular." "I will spend my entire salary so that I can't meet my payments, and then the bank will cut off my credit and close my account." "I'll develop diseases that are hard to cure" (such as anorexia).

Physical symptoms: Guilt feelings in the body are located in the kidneys (pangs of conscience), hence these people may suffer from problems in the urinary tract, cancer of the bladder, prostate problems, problems with the uterus, and various forms of self-punishment. There is also the possibility of digestive problems, because they do not digest things properly.

Pine is good for treating compulsive eaters. It can calm them down, reducing the need for self-flagellation. It is good for children whose parents are in the throes of divorce, when they are being used as a bargaining chip, and feel guilty for having to "choose" one of the parents; for people who work themselves half to death; for people who sacrifice themselves in a relationship, particularly women; for people who do not know how to give and receive in a balanced manner; for problems with having sexual relations based on a feeling of internal guilt, sado-masochism.

25. Red Chestnut

Red Chestnut is used for treating exaggerated conditions of anxiety and worry about future disasters that may befall the person and those close to him. Sometimes this is manifested outwardly by interference in the life of a loved one (a child, for example) out of fear that something is going to happen to him.

Characteristic sentences: "I rang your office because I wasn't sure if you were involved in the traffic accident they mentioned on the news or not." "You didn't arrive on time, so I thought you'd been hurt in a gang war."

This is a very troublesome energy, which is not only accompanied by very severe negative thoughts, but courts disaster. When a tragedy does happen, people of this type say "You see?" "I told you so." "Now tell me that I don't have to worry - it's a fact; look what happened."

The essence is calming, enabling the person to see the unreality of his fears. Gradually these things stop preoccupying him (he forgets about them), and he shows more confidence and faith in those around him and in life itself.

26. Rock Rose

Rock Rose is a first-aid essence for treating situations of panic, such as after accidents or receiving bad news. It is also effective after a serious illness. The action of the essence is immediate, and it quickly calms the situation down. It is a good essence for all the side effects of panic, such as the hair rapidly turning white as a result of shock, or losing hair all over the body as a result of terrible fear (not alopecia due to a severe illness or hormonal imbalance). The essence is also good for women in childbirth. The essence neutralizes panic immediately.

27. Rock Water

Rock Water is an essence for treating people who are hard on themselves, and as a result suffer from a lack of self-esteem. They measure themselves against a very harsh yardstick, and consequently never feel satisfied with themselves. They impose a strict regime of self-discipline, repression, and self-denial on themselves. They aspire to be an example and a role model to others, while inside themselves they yearn to feel *joie de vivre*, freedom, and spontaneity.

The essence helps them to be less hard on themselves, and almost without noticing it, they let up a bit and allow themselves to be freer.

28. Scleranthus

Scleranthus helps people in decision-making and is appropriate for situations in which people vacillate between two alternatives and are unable to decide. As a type, these are people who waver, and have a hard time deciding to do something or not, to decide or not to decide. Sometimes, because they are unable to decide, they never begin to act. These types are also liable to be very fickle - to the point of hypocrisy - and prone to extreme mood swings.

Physical symptoms: Problems with balance, a tendency to faint, vertigo, a feeling of instability, insomnia, alternating episodes of constipation and diarrhea, appetite or lack of appetite.

29. Star of Bethlehem

Star of Bethlehem treats conditions of shock, trauma, collapse after hearing bad news; it is for used for treating traumas and serves as first aid for injuries, fainting spells, traffic accidents and so on, as well as before and after operations.

The essence is layered - it cleanses in a layered fashion, starting with the upper levels and working its way down to the depths. Used over the long term, the essence may raise traumas up into the conscious level in order to give the person a chance to cope with them correctly. The essence also cures infections, and is efficient as a rub for fractures, wounds, and hemorrhages.

30. Sweet Chestnut

Sweet Chestnut is used for treating conditions of bitterness, melancholy, terrible, deep despair, and tremendous, hopeless agonies of the soul. It is appropriate in moments of crisis when the person feels that there are no solutions to situations in which it seems as though he has been utterly abandoned and isolated, a feeling of no way out, of no more strength, and an incapacity to deal with anything else. The essence cleans up the emotional debris immediately, "lifting" the person and enveloping him.

31. Vervain

This is an essence for people who direct all their energies toward a given goal or toward extremism and fanaticism about a cause of some kind, to the point of coercing those around them. The type is likely to be characterized by tremendous will power and leadership ability, and he harnesses those around him to the cause that he champions.

In a situation of imbalance, he is likely to go overboard in his missionary zeal to the extent of getting into confrontations. These types expend a great deal of energy without balancing their internal energy, so they burn up a lot of energy and strength. The essence is also appropriate in instances of blind faith in a given thing to the point that the person harms himself for the sake of the "objective."

The essence can be beneficial in bedwetting among older children, protracted diarrhea, and hyperactivity.

Physical symptoms: Irritability, difficulty in falling asleep, weakened immune system, tight muscles, headaches, stiff body.

32. Vine

Vine is used for treating people who are very domineering and tyrannical toward those around them, and totally lacking in flexibility. They are sometimes violent and abusive toward the people around them. These people only feel strong when they can define the other person as weaker than they, and may even attempt to make that happen. These people do not argue: they lay down the law and make it clear with a look or with violent behavior that their demands must be met. Vine is often appropriate for people in the military and law enforcement who continue doing their job at home as well.

Characteristic sentences: "You will do what I say, right now, and without any argument!" "Forget about 'why' - I said so and that's that!"

This essence is very suitable for adolescence, for children who control the house, and for people who have gained power and status and exploit this fact mercilessly.

Physical symptoms: Constipation, stiffness in the joints, high blood pressure, migraines.

A few drops in coffee or tea each day, and the person will gradually become more gentle and understanding. It works miracles, if one can only convince the person to take the essence. (Some people administer it without the person knowing, which is legitimate in view of the reign of terror that prevails in the home).

33. Walnut

Walnut is known as the "breaker of bonds." It gets a person out of the rut of a particular way of thinking, removes the evil eye, protects and assists in breaking habits, and is very effective against addictions of all sorts. It is very important for therapists who absorb energies from their patients.

It is good for use in the following situations: For treatment of people who are influenced by a power stronger than themselves such as a personality, ties with the past, memories, habits, against the evil eye, for use during a period of transition (any transitional period in life at any age and situation: teething, toilet training, moving house, separation, and so on), for any situation of breaking an addiction or habit. It helps in situations of remorse and broken-heartedness. It works on three levels: Breaking loose from the past; protection - it gives the person a sense of being enveloped in a transparent protective bubble so that he can examine the situation in an objective manner, without emotional turmoil and without being hurt; and it eases transitions.

It is beneficial for those who are oversensitive and require protection; for people who have a tendency to create symbiotic relationships - with friends, family, workmates, and so forth - which contain a destructive element; for people who need to travel and have a hard time letting go; and for children who cling to their mother.

Physical symptoms: According to the particular case.

34. Water Violet

Water Violet is used for treating people who withdraw and keep apart from their surroundings, so that they are sometimes considered aloof. Their inner feeling is that they are a cut above other people, and for that reason, they prefer to be by themselves. They have a very strong presence, they are dominant, and other people feel very small beside them. They are independent and deep, but have a hard time expressing and demonstrating emotions; they detest emotional outbursts and shy away from physical contact. It is hard to get them excited. They are not hedonists, nor are they spontaneous. When they are called up on the telephone, they always sound as if they have been disturbed; their answers are curt. They do not have many friends; they are cold, emotionally cool types. It is likely that a situation of this sort results from fear, trauma, and lack of love. It could be that as a child, the person learned very quickly that if he didn't look out for himself, no one else would look out for him. Perhaps he learned that feeling is dangerous and that forming relationships with people means pain. People of this type sometimes had difficult childhood experiences of abandonment or rejection by a parent in their past.

Physical symptoms: Problems with the blood vessels, arteriosclerosis, hemorrhoids, problems with the digestive system, particularly constipation, ulcers, joint inflammations, slipped discs, muscle problems, migraines, dermatological problems (if they don't let it out, it comes out through the skin).

35. White Chestnut

White Chestnut helps situations in which a person feels that his head is buzzing with thoughts, ranging from a song on the radio that he keeps hearing over and over in his head all day, to bothersome thoughts that preoccupy him. He cannot function properly and does not manage to get to sleep. The essence is good for insomnia that is caused by worrisome thoughts. Sometimes the situation is accompanied by overanxiety. These people sometimes talk to or argue with themselves, and they fail to hear what's going on around them because of the internal din. The essence is also good before meditation, as it calms the flow of thoughts.

Physical symptoms: Headaches, earaches, ringing in the ears, migraines, problems with the shoulders and neck, which are usually knotted up.

Characteristic sentences: "I hear my thoughts inside my head" - as though they hear the wheels turning inside their head.

36. Wild Oat

Wild Oat is appropriate for talented, ambitious, and multifaceted types who are not able to decide what to do with their lives because of their inability to focus on a limited number of areas only. These people are liable to move from profession to profession, learn numerous things superficially, and experience constant frustration and dissatisfaction.

The essence also improves the ability to concentrate and make decisions. It helps the person find his vocation and his path in life, and to stay there, without wandering off in too many directions.

37. Wild Rose

Wild Rose is an essence for treating conditions of apathy, indifference, being in a rut, and fear of change and the processes of change. It is suitable for people who refuse to accept the fact that they themselves created the situation and that they are the ones who are allowing it to deteriorate; for people who have become apathetic following great suffering; for people who live an unenjoyable routine, but don't have the strength to get up and change it.

Characteristic sentences: "I have to learn to live with this." "That's how it is in life." "It's a hereditary disease; there's nothing that can be done."

38. Willow

Willow is an essence for treating people who are bitter, who are constantly whining, who feel that everyone owes them because they are unfortunate and deprived. They do not know how to feel gratitude, but nurture feelings of deprivation and bitterness, and complain incessantly. They perceive themselves as victims, becoming bitter, resentful, and depressed. Because of these traits, people tend to avoid them, and they don't understand that they are the ones who are creating this situation.

Characteristic sentences: "I don't deserve this." "It isn't fair." "I always get gypped."

39. Rescue Remedy

This is a first-aid remedy for every situation - immediately following a trauma, a traffic accident, receiving bad news, or the like. It is also effective in any situation of nervousness, such as before an exam, test, or important meeting where the person feels that he's quaking with fear. It is good in any situation of temporary emotional upset, fright, anxiety, collapse, panic, shock, irritability, hysteria, violent outbursts, severe confusion, faintness, and loss of consciousness. The remedy consists of five Bach Flower essences: Star of Bethlehem, Clematis, Cherry Plum, Impatiens, and Rock Rose. It works quickly and effectively, and it should always be kept on hand.

Astrolog Publishing House
P. O. Box 1123, Hod Hasharon 45111, Israel
Tel: 972-9-7412044
Fax: 972-9-7442714
E-Mail: info@astrolog.co.il
Astrolog Web Site: www.astrolog.co.il

Copyright © Susan Holden 2000

ISBN 965-494-113-9

All rights reserved. No part of this publication may
be reproduced, stored in a retrieval system, or
transmitted, in any form or by any means, electronic,
mechanical, photocopying, recording or otherwise,
without the prior permission of the publisher.

Published by Astrolog Publishing House 2000

Printed in Israel
2 4 6 8 10 9 7 5 3 1